Original title:
Searching for Meaning with a GPS

Copyright © 2025 Creative Arts Management OÜ
All rights reserved.

Author: Alec Donovan
ISBN HARDBACK: 978-1-80566-089-7
ISBN PAPERBACK: 978-1-80566-384-3

Routes to the Soul's Inquiry

I punched in my dreams, with a hopeful sigh,
But the voice said, "Recalculating," oh why oh why?
My heart mapped a course, so straightforward,
Yet somehow led me to the snack aisle, oh lord!

The Journey Beyond the Waypoints

Turn left at the cactus, then right at the sun,
I swear I knew the way; this can't be fun!
A detour through life's maze, I seem to get lost,
Might as well grab a taco before I pay the cost.

Uncharted Territories of Thought

With pins on my brain like a visual feast,
A treasure map drawn by a benevolent beast.
But alas, my directions led me in circles,
And all I found was a flock of weird turtles.

Turning the Dial of Destiny

Tap left for the wisdom, tap right for the woe,
Can someone fix the dial? It won't let me go!
A twist here, a fumble, navigating the day,
In search of bright banners but tripping on gray.

Points of Light Amidst Darkness

In the dark, I press 'go',
The screen lights up my face,
But the route is all wrong,
Now I'm lost in cyberspace.

Turn left at the taco stand,
A right by the dancing gnome,
I might find enlightenment,
Or just a weird old dome.

Cartography of the Soul

My heart's a tangled map,
With lines that lead astray,
A detour through the ice cream shop,
Has beamed me all day.

Coordinates scribbled on a napkin,
Lead to paths of pure delight,
Where joy and laughter intersect,
Underneath the neon light.

Navigating the Labyrinth of Life

At life's crossroads, I pause,
With choices left and right,
The little arrow spins around,
Am I lost? Oh, what a sight!

I took a left at 'Chicken Wing',
Then zoomed by 'Land of Cheese',
If only my GPS could talk,
It'd say, 'Just take it easy, please.'

Signals Lost in the Wilderness

In the woods, my phone went dead,
I waved it like a wand,
With no connection to my brain,
I guess I must respond.

A squirrel gave me directions,
Climbing high up in a tree,
'Just follow the breadcrumbs, friend,
And perhaps drink some tea!'

Labyrinths of Introspection

In a maze where thoughts collide,
I wander lost, but with great pride.
My mind's a map, but oh so bent,
   Directions lead me to the rent.

Turn left at 'why' and right at 'how',
I swear I knew much more back now.
Each twist and turn, a giggle here,
   My inner compass lost all cheer.

Charting the Course to Inner Calm

With a guide that knows no bounds,
I drift through joy, where silence sounds.
A route marked 'zen' just popped up bright,
But is it left or right tonight?

I swear I heard a traffic beep,
Maybe life's a jest, not deep.
With every step, my feet do dance,
To find my calm, I'd need a chance.

A Voyage Through the Ether

Sailing waves of hopes and fears,
On a boat of laughter, sailing cheers.
The GPS says go straight ahead,
But it forgot the 'turns' I dread.

I squint at clouds for signs from fate,
But all it gives is a comedy plate.
Through storms of thought, I float along,
Hoping the laughter's where I belong.

The Unseen Journey of the Heart

My heart's a journey, wild and free,
With exits marked, 'fool' and 'me'.
I tick the box for 'don't know how',
As love's direction gives a wow.

With each mile logged and laugh set loose,
I find my way like goofball moose.
The road is bumpy, full of quirks,
But joy is found in silly works.

Tracking Shadows on the Ground

Lost in a field, my phone went blank,
The sun was bright, my vision sank.
Shadows danced, like crazy fools,
I traced them back with all my tools.

I laughed at the map, upside-down,
Pointing south while I faced town.
A cow looked up, gave me a glance,
'Just follow me,' it said, in a prance.

Paths That Cross and Diverge

Two paths forked in the woods one day,
One led to snacks, the other, a stray.
With laughter loud, I took a bite,
'Who needs purpose?' I joked, feeling light.

My friend yelled loud, 'Let's turn around!'
But I walked on, munching, spellbound.
The map in my hand was quite absurd,
But I followed my nose, not a word heard.

The Quest for Purpose in Coordinates

A button clicked, with confidence bright,
The screen glowed back, directing my flight.
Coordinates drew like a colorful map,
But all I found was a huge old chap.

He scratched his beard, then grinned wide,
'The meaning of life is a fun joyride!'
I checked my GPS, felt it was wrong,
But we laughed and sat, it didn't take long.

Where GPS Meets the Mind's Eye

Tech in hand, I thought I was led,
Each wrong turn filled me with dread.
My device insisted I was fine,
But led me straight to a garden of pine.

With squirrels laughing, I questioned my fate,
Could the squirrels help me navigate?
Lost in laughter, I found a new route,
With joy in my heart, I began to scoot.

Harmony in Digital Noise

In a world of chirps and beeps,
I set my course, but oh, it creeps!
With my phone in hand, I take a chance,
While dodging street lamps in a dance.

"Recalculating!" the voice calls out,
As I drive around in circles, no doubt.
Did I miss a turn or lose my mind?
At least the pizza won't get declined!

The Thread That Guides Us

Invisible strings in a tech-filled world,
Like kittens untangled, laughter unfurled.
A map of emotions that ebbs and flows,
As we zigzag through life where chaos grows.

Follow the dot, oh so shiny and bright,
But it leads to the wrong store, what a sight!
With a wink and a chuckle, we'll find our way,
With coffee and friendship, come what may!

As We Map Our Own Destiny

With a thumb on the screen and dreams in our head,
We're out to discover what's lurking ahead.
Turn left at the laughter, then right by the fun,
GPS giggles, the adventure's begun!

"Arrive at destination!" she sings with a grin,
But the place isn't here; it's a hair salon spin!
We fashion our way with humor to share,
In a world of directions, we rarely despair!

Shifting Grounds of Navigation

With devices ablaze, our direction is set,
Yet my buddy insists we're not there yet!
He proclaims, "These roads must be cursed or confused!"

As we dodge the detours, slightly bemused.

Through fog and confusion our laughter rings clear,
In this digital maze, we shed our fear.
Getting lost is a journey; what a delight,
As we laugh at the chaos, navigating the night!

The Map of Unseen Paths

In a sea of squiggly lines, I roam,
Waving my phone like a magic dome.
Turn left at the cat and right by the tree,
Who knew my next turn would lead to a bee?

Coffee cups scattered, crumbs on the way,
Navigating life like I swerve in my sway.
An arrow spins wildly, it's lost in the fray,
"Oh look, a giraffe!?" I shout in dismay.

Coordinates of the Heart

Pinch of the screen, it vibrates with glee,
Where's my soulmate? Is he hiding in a tree?
Latitude? Longitude? My heart's in a twist,
Why do all the best ones seem like a myth?

I sent out a beacon, 'Come find me, dear!
Between the couch cushions, I know you are near.
With a tap and a swipe, it's romance I seek,
But land me a date, not a schedule with bleak.

Finding North in the Unknown

Lost in the jungle of online delight,
GPS says turn left – I can't see the light.
My compass spins round like a child on a ride,
'Where's the taco stand?' I ask with great pride.

"To reach your destination, just follow your nose,"
But it leads me to pickles and shoes, I suppose.
Charting strange waters, my ship's in a whirl,
Finding true north? It's a game with a twirl.

Echoes of the Silent Compass

A whispering needle, my sanity lost,
On the map, it scribbles, at what a cost?
"I swear, it's right here!" I cry to the stars,
But all I can find are a million old cars.

In the land of detours, my patience runs thin,
Every bend and twist feels like losing a twin.
Giggles escape, as I spin in the void,
Finding my path is like finding a toy.

Seeking the Horizon in Digital Dusk

I set my sights on clouds so high,
With a click and a tap, my thoughts can fly.
But the signal fades, and I start to roam,
Is this a journey or a digital poem?

In twilight's glow, fun leads the way,
Maps upside down, oh what a display!
Stumbled on landmarks of silicon dreams,
Where my phone tells me nothing, or so it seems.

Lost and Found in Data Streams

I tried to find Waldo in the code,
But all I found was a heavy load.
The GPS giggles, takes a wrong turn,
Leaving my head in a digital churn.

Flags pop up like weeds on the screen,
Directions unclear, if you know what I mean.
'Left at the next feature,' it said with glee,
But I ended up lost in the vast binary sea.

Unraveling the Web of Existence

I clicked on a link, it spun and twirled,
Unraveling threads of a chaotic world.
One page leads to another and what a maze,
Lost in the web's captivating haze.

With every click, I laugh and sigh,
This map knows me better than I know why.
Caught in a loop, around I go,
Is the truth out there? Well, I don't know!

Milestones in the Quest for Clarity

I set my goals as bright as the stars,
But my path's unclear, filled with digital scars.
Every stop a milestone, quirky and neat,
Yet clarity hides under cookies and tweets.

My compass spins wildly, pointing to shows,
Detours through memes, who knows where it goes?
With laughter, I ponder this outrageous ride,
Unraveling curiosities, I can't let slide.

The Riddle of the Route

In a car with friends, we chase the sun,
Our map is a puzzle, oh what fun!
Is that a left or right, we can't decide,
Like a blindfolded race, we take each stride.

A shortcut turns into a wild goose chase,
We find ourselves lost in this curious place.
Laughter echoes through the winding way,
Every wrong turn adds more to the play.

Unmarked Paths of Discovery

We ventured off-grid, oh what a sight,
With no signs to guide, we laugh in delight.
Each twist and each turn feels like a dream,
Lost in translation, yet full of steam.

Remember the road marked with chicken coops?
Every detour leads to the craziest loops.
Maps are for losers, we yell in cheer,
Finding our way with each giggle and jeer.

Flickers on the Horizon

At the horizon, we spot a strange gleam,
Is it a mirage or part of our dream?
With snacks in the back, we take a bold plunge,
What's out there? Another mystery to unbrunge!

The GPS nags, 'Recalculate!' it whines,
But who needs a plan when adventure aligns?
We laugh at the 'wrong' turns we have made,
In the chaos of routes, our joy won't fade.

Unfolding the Fabric of Purpose

In the fabric of paths, we stitch and we sew,
With threads of confusion, let spontaneity flow.
Who knew that a coffee shop would surprise?
With pastries and quirks, it's fuel for the rise!

Every detour we take is a patch in our quilt,
A reminder of laughter, not marred by guilt.
So here's to the maps that go wildly astray,
For in every wrong turn, we find our own way!

Circles of Reflection

I wander down the road so wide,
With a gadget that's my trusted guide.
It spins and twirls like a dizzy kite,
Yet where is home, not quite in sight.

Turn left, turn right, oh what a game,
It leads me around, I'm feeling the same.
I'm lost in laughter, can't find the way,
Though my GPS sings, just for today.

The Voyage Within

My device beeps loud, what's that all about?
"Make a U-turn!" it starts to shout.
I look around, lost in the fun,
What's a destination? I've hardly begun!

"Recalculating," it chortles and jokes,
Mimicking the sounds made by quirky folks.
In this winding quest where I try to roam,
I find my laughter, and that feels like home.

Trails of Understanding

I follow the route like a clueless hare,
Bumping into squirrels, but I don't care.
With trees for landmarks, I'm feeling wise,
Nature laughs softly, wearing a surprise.

"Take the next exit," the voice cheerfully brays,
But I'm dancing in circles, just lost in a maze.
Each step's a riddle, a comic delight,
Who knew getting lost could feel so right?

Finding Footing in Flux

The map's a jumble, the compass spins,
I'm more confused than the state of my bins.
With every wrong turn, I giggle and frown,
Who knew this journey would turn me around?

"Arriving soon," it says with a smirk,
But I'm in a park, and all I do is lurk.
Chasing my tail, but never too far,
I'll find my way home - it's just bizarre!

The Language of Lost Signals

In a world where arrows twirl,
My phone's a compass, yet it swirls.
It says I'm close, then takes a dive,
Am I alive or just a drive?

The blue dot blinks, a wily tease,
Is that the road or just some trees?
Turn left at laughter, right at screams,
Navigating life or just my dreams?

Unveiling Patterns in the Confusion

Maps in hand, I strut with flair,
Each turn I take is full of care.
A detour here, a joyride there,
Why do directions make me swear?

With every reroute, I see the light,
But wait! Was that a left or right?
Laughing as I trip on plots,
Where's my tea and parking spots?

The Mapmaker's Dream

Sketching routes in the dead of night,
A map that's blurred, but feels so right.
With every squiggle, my heart does race,
How did I end up at this strange place?

X marks the spot where I lost my pen,
I could have sworn I'd been here then.
The map whispers secrets, quite a tease,
I'm lost but happy—oh, what a breeze!

A Voyage Through the Intersection

At crossroads, I dance with glee,
Which way to go? Oh, let's just see!
One path leads to muffins, that sounds grand,
Wait, do I need to check my planned?

Each turn's a giggle, laughter shared,
Adventures waiting, I'm unprepared.
Missed the exit? Here's a pun,
My journey grows richer, hey, this is fun!

Circling Back to Where We Began

I turned left, then I turned right,
But somehow I lost my sight.
The map says 'Home,' I say 'Maybe,'
At this rate I'll be the next McGrady!

I recalibrate, press 'start' anew,
Yet end up at Lou's instead of you.
The trees wave 'hi,' the signs just laugh,
Following this path, I need a new craft!

With each twist, I question fate,
Is destiny deciding my state?
I'll trade my GPS for a magic wand,
But even Houdini might not respond!

Oh, the irony of my little quest,
Each wrong turn feels like a jest.
Maps under my pillow, dreams in the air,
But follow this route? I think I'll just stare!

Aligning Stars with the Compass

I flipped my compass and it went wild,
No North, just chaos, I'm mildly riled.
The stars are laughing; they know my plight,
My trusty GPS thinks it's a flight!

In search of direction with such grand intent,
My compass spins like it's heaven-sent.
I'm headed 'off-road,' the scariest scheme,
This journey could end up in a meme!

Like chasing a rainbow, I trot and glide,
But in what dimension does my ship reside?
Each tick of the dial spins a brand new tale,
I'd be better off trying to sail!

So to the heavens, I look for clues,
With a wink from the cosmos, there's nothing to lose.
I'll dance with the stars, in this cosmic mess,
Compass or not, I'll just guess!

Where Do We Go From Here?

Rerouting, rerouting, it's a funny scene,
My car's a disco, with all these screens.
Do I turn left, right, or straight take a chance?
The GPS says 'light up'—what a romance!

Each wrong turn plays a cue to my tune,
Is that a cow on a road like a cartoon?
Traffic signs giggle, as I go astray,
Maybe detours are just games to play.

The portable voice says, 'Turn back, dear,'
But I'm laughing at life, it's all crystal clear.
With a grin on my face, I'll blaze my own trail,
Who knew getting lost could be such a tale?

So where do we go? It's all part of the dance,
With every wrong turn, I'm still in my prance.
I'll embrace the adventure, the map's a ruse,
In the zany world, I've got nothing to lose!

Reflections in the Rearview Mirror

In the mirror, I see my past blurs,
Waving goodbye to my own little furs.
Every intersection a wild surprise,
Navigating life with a pair of wide eyes!

Oh, the roads I've taken, where do they lead?
A comical puzzle, like trying to breed.
I chuckle aloud at the routes that I've made,
When will this awkward journey ever fade?

Each mile a lesson, a tone, a quirk,
Navigating through life's playful work.
Reflecting on laughter I leave in my wake,
But where's the fun in just being opaque?

So here I am, in the driver's seat,
With my GPS glitch turning joy into feat.
Life is too short for a straight-laced affair,
In circles we wander, with giggles to spare!

Pixels and Possibilities

A map of pixels bright and bold,
With routes outlined in tales untold.
I tap and swipe, then make a turn,
Yet still to find what I must learn.

My phone, it sings with joy, oh glee,
But sends me to a clown with a tree.
He juggles dreams while balloons fly high,
I laugh and sigh, oh me, oh my!

A turn here, a change of track,
Sometimes I wander, sometimes I hack.
The GPS thinks it knows what's right,
But leads me to a pizza at midnight!

In pixels bright, I chase a fate,
Yet find the best when I just wait.
With laughter as my guiding star,
I'll wander far, oh yes, I spar!

Lost Signals in the Noise

Amidst the chatter, static, and zest,
The signals get crossed, it's quite the jest.
I ask for directions, get told to dance,
And switch from the road to a game of chance.

The voice in my phone is peppy and bright,
But sends me off into a cactus fight.
I could swear I asked for a left turn here,
But end up at a llama, munching on beer.

I shout at the screen, 'You silly old thing!
Why lead me away from the pizza king?'
Yet laughter ensues as I gallivant,
With lost signals, I'll yet make them chant.

The noise of the world blends into one song,
Where I skip along, can't help but belong.
So if I get lost, hey, that's okay,
With laughter as my guide, I'll find my way!

Recalculating Dreams

The voice announces, 'Recalculating!'
While I'm here, totally contemplating.
A dream detour, how quirky and fun,
Who knew life's paths weren't just one run?

With each recalculation, I giggle and grin,
Who knew a wrong turn could lead to such win?
I find treasures in places I'd never expect,
Like running into a cat with a crown and a check.

'In 100 feet, turn left,' it claims,
But I find myself amid wild llama games.
I join in their dance, shining like a star,
While my GPS mutters, 'You've gone too far.'

Yet in this mischief, a magic is found,
With dreams recalibrated, joy knows no bounds.
The road is a canvas, a playful spree,
I laugh at the journey, just let it be!

The Road Less Traveled

Upon the road less taken, I cheer,
With twists and turns and a bit of fear.
The GPS thinks it knows the best,
But off I go, to the wild west.

Through fields of giggles and streams of fun,
I chase the sun, oh look, there's a bun!
I thought I'd find wisdom at the end of this path,
Instead, I met a duck with a bubble bath.

Each bump in the road is a laugh I can share,
With friends who wander, beyond any care.
If I stray from the route, hey, what's the cost?
In this ridiculous journey, never am I lost.

So bring on the detours, the wrong turns, the spree,
For every misstep is just meant to be.
With joy on my face and a twinkling eye,
The road less traveled is my favorite sky!

A Journey of Infinite Directions

In a car with wheels so round,
I drive clueless through the town.
The screen says "turn around, my friend"
But my adventure will not end.

A route that twists, a path that bends,
Each twist and turn just never ends.
"Recalculating," it starts to whine,
I guess that means I'm doing fine.

GPS hums with all its might,
While I just smile at my plight.
Maps are old, they're yesterday's chat,
I'll just trust my loyal cat.

So onward I go, a brave explorer,
With snacks galore and a dance to bore.
Who knows what I'll find out there?
Maybe a llama, or a jungle lair.

Through the Maze of the Unknown

In a maze built by Google's map,
I zigzag like I'm in a trap.
"Turn left," it cries, "no wait, go right!"
My joyrides turn into a fright.

A route that's supposed to be clear,
Has set me adrift with plenty of beer.
Each twist and turn makes my head spin,
At this rate, I'll never win.

"Destination!" it wails in glee,
But I see naught but a giant tree.
Is this the forest of lost phone calls?
Or do I just prefer these walls?

With laughter and snacks, I won't frown,
Getting lost is my new hometown.
In this labyrinth where I roam,
I've found the best kind of home.

Hints of Meaning in the GPS Void

In a galaxy of blinking lights,
The GPS shows its great delights.
A beep here, a ping there,
Is it guiding? I'm just unaware.

"Turn in 500 feet," it chirps so bright,
But where, oh where is the path so right?
Each bump and curve brings more dismay,
Is it a map or games we play?

Directions lost in a sea of tech,
I ask my friend who gives a peck.
"Just drive straight, and then you'll see,
A coffee shop, just wait for me!"

So on I go with a voice that's sassy,
This trip has turned rather classy.
GPS jests, I'm in for the fun,
Maybe we'll end up in the sun!

A Tapestry of Navigational Stars

In a car powered by starlight dreams,
I cruise along on shimmering beams.
The navigation waves like a flag,
While I dance in my comfy rag.

"Recalculating," it says with glee,
I thought we agreed on a cup of tea!
Every detour brings a new treat,
I smell pastries baking, oh isn't life sweet?

With every signal lost, I grin wide,
This journey is the best joyride.
Maps mean little when spirits are high,
So off I go, beneath the sky.

Through laughter and snacks, we journey afar,
With a laugh, a giggle, we are the stars.
The joy isn't found in the end of the line,
But in the antics, oh dear, so divine!

In Pursuit of Waypoints

I turned left at the big red barn,
But my map said, "Oh, what a yarn!"
A goat crossed my path, wearing a hat,
I just wanted to find my way back to chat.

With arrows that spin and voices that beep,
It's like a treasure hunt through fields of sheep.
"Recalculating" is my new best friend,
I swear it just wants to drive me 'round the bend.

So here I am, on this winding lane,
Following breadcrumbs, but losing my brain.
A signpost points straight but I go left,
Life's a comedy; I'm just a bit bereft.

Yet in this merry mess of twists and turns,
I find a giggle where my heart still yearns.
For every plummet, there's a soaring flight,
Maybe getting lost just feels so right!

Signals in the Static

A voice crackles through my brand new phone,
"Take a U-turn, you're all alone."
I laugh out loud, the map's quite a sport,
Who knew directions could be such a court?

I've found a café, though it's marked as closed,
The GPS must think it's cleverly dozed.
I sip my coffee and ponder the stars,
Maybe even roadmap's lost in its own bars.

"Make a sharp left!" echoes in my ear,
As I bump into someone I hold dear.
It seems that getting lost isn't all bad,
It led me to memories that I once had.

So laugh with me as I take a wrong track,
Let's toast to the moments that bring us back.
Signals may falter, my path may get hazy,
But together it's always a fun kind of crazy!

Between Directions and Dilemmas

I aimed for the beach, but wound up in town,
All because my phone likes to mess around.
It said, "Follow the road, make a right at the cat,"
I found a big dog. Oh, fancy that!

My coffee went cold as I parked by a tree,
The map's more confused than it shows to me.
"Stay on the path" is its favorite line,
But I've driven in circles since a quarter to nine.

Each turn is an adventure, each wrong seems right,
My sanity waved like a kite in full flight.
Behind every corner, surprises galore,
Like running into Uncle Joe at the corner store.

But isn't it funny, this trip of a spree?
Life, like my GPS, won't stop teasing me.
To dance with directions and whims all day,
Perhaps getting lost is just here to stay!

The Echoes of Lost Frequencies

I heard a beep and I jumped in my seat,
"Your destination is on the street!"
But all I can see is a cow on the lane,
Who knew a detour could be such a pain?

The clouds formed arrows, or so I thought,
Leading me to places that I surely fought.
With lyrics buffering through my radio's tone,
I've lost two hours but found a ghost town.

"Turn left at the llama," a voice does declare,
But I'm not sure if it's pulling my hair.
It's not a drive—it's a laugh-filled ride,
With each wrong choice, I let joy be my guide.

So here's to the chaos, let's celebrate!
Maps lose their step, but I find my fate.
Amid the giggles and splendid mishaps,
I've discovered that joy is where laughter naps.

Between Turns and False Starts

I followed the map, it led me astray,
In circles I drove, what a silly display.
A left where it said, I ended up right,
My GPS giggled, oh what a sight!

"Recalculating," it said with a wink,
As I navigated madness, I started to think.
Where is this place? Oh, where could it be?
The landmarks are fading, just like my sanity!

Each turn is a gamble, a chance for a laugh,
Past fields of confusion, I need a good calf.
"Turn left in five hundred," it chirps with glee,
But I'm lost in a maze with no exit to see!

A detour through chaos, for info I'd barter,
The journey of life, oh how I do trotter!
Maps may confound, and roads may mislead,
But this ride is a joy, oh yes, indeed!

Constellations on the Route to Discovery

In my car, I'm a stargazer, mapping my fate,
The stars are misguiding, can't be this late!
A tour of the cosmos from the driver's seat,
But my roadside astrology is far from neat.

Finding the Milky Way took way too long,
I got lost in a roundabout, how could that be wrong?
"Just follow the sun," my co-pilot said wise,
But I ended up facing a barbecue surprise!

Planets and satellites lit up the road,
Yet my GPS plotted a very odd code.
"Fork left at the comet," who knew that would steer,
To a taco truck party, now that I can cheer!

The map of the heavens won a round of applause,
Though I wound up in traffic, I'll do it because
Every bump in the road's a bright shooting star,
And stumbling to laughter is the best way to go far!

The Trail of Thought and Time

They say life's a journey, a winding old track,
Yet my trusty old app just led me off black.
A shortcut through thought, or a pitstop at fate?
My mind's a maze, in the world of debate.

"Proceed to the route," it tells me with pride,
While I'm busy reflecting on the choices I hide.
But the road keeps twisting, like my thoughts on parade,
Who knew pondering life would have me delayed?

Contradictions await at the next intersection,
Do I veer left to wisdom, or right to distraction?
The speed bumps of logic pop up like candy,
And navigating feelings? Oh, that's just dandy!

Just take me to lunch, I'll ponder my head,
With fries as companions, I'll savor the spread.
Each turn brings a chuckle, each bump adds a tale,
This journey is madness, but I sure love the trail!

Digital Breadcrumbs in the Wilderness

In the woods, I'm a breadcrumb, lost but not meek,
With pixels to guide me, though they take a peek.
"Head north," it instructed, "You'll find your way home,"

But instead, I got sidetracked by a garden gnome!

I swiped left on a river, right turned to muck,
The closer I got, just less sense and more luck.
My screen flashed directions, like it knew it all well,
But I'm caught in a thicket, in this green leafy cell.

Every beep from the device gives a chuckle or groan,
"Recalculating," it grins while I chase a brown bone.
Lost in the foliage, with pixie dust all around,
I'm just another wanderer, laughter's the sound.

So here's to the journey, with laughter in tow,
Each misstep a riot, oh what a show!
I'll follow those breadcrumbs wherever they lead,
For the wilderness whispers, and adventure's the creed!

The Beacon Beyond the Fog

In the mist, I drive around,
Maps are where lost hopes are found.
The voice says, 'Turn right, not left!'
But all I find is one big cleft.

My phone's a pro, or so it claims,
Yet I'm still playing car roulette games.
'Rerouting' sounds like a bad date,
While I circle the same block—what fate!

The lights twinkle like stars above,
As I fumble with directions I don't love.
A pizza sign leads me astray,
But at least I'm getting food today!

Finally, a spot where I can park,
I scream, 'GPS, you're such a lark!'
But deep down I know it's just my way,
Of turning journeys into a fray.

A Chorus of Signs

Walking down the street with glee,
Every sign yells out at me.
'No U-turns? What a bore!'
But a taco truck sells dreams galore.

I squint at directions, what a sight,
'You have arrived!'—but that can't be right.
A parking lot? Where's the fun?
I wanted a beach, not a run.

The map flips upside down with style,
Two lefts, a right—oops, walked a mile.
'Fooled ya!' says my cheerful app,
Jumping from puddles like a happy chap.

And as I dance past every billboard,
I chase clues with a sprightly sword.
In a world of whimsy, I reside,
With every step, a twisty ride.

Serendipity in the Sidebar

Scroll down the screen, a quest so funny,
Charting my course for a bit of honey.
'Head southwest at the next green bush,'
But I end up lost with a silly shush.

Emails pop up; they want my soul,
While I'm just trying to find my role.
Branches entangled, what a sight—
Maybe I'll just take off and take flight.

Click. Clack. Error sounds ease my mind,
As I giggle at every unkind.
It's a circus of fun, this digital spree,
Finding a burger joint sounds good to me!

I stumble and trip through virtual schemes,
Every wrong turn bursts at the seams.
In the sidebar where laughter's born,
I'll find some joy by the time I'm worn.

Threading Through the Void

In the void I float with grace,
Looking for a familiar place.
A ping, a beep, an upbeat song,
Tells me I've been lost too long.

Cloudy with a chance of lost ideas,
I toggle buttons, void the fears.
A wormhole here, a detour there,
Navigating life like I'm on a dare.

Poking at maps like a child at play,
Am I going forward or back? I sway.
Each twist and turn serves up a laugh,
Life's a puzzle, I'll take the gaffe.

So guide me home, oh GPS friend,
On this wobbly road, where all paths end.
A journey of giggles, missteps, and cheer,
Navigating through voids—what a frontier!

Charting the Unseen

In this realm where arrows roam,
I tap and tap to find my home.
But the screen spins like a dizzy round,
And I'm lost in circles, feet on the ground.

With points of interest leading astray,
I chase them all, what a grand display!
The hot dog stand, the coffee shop line,
Turns out, I'm quite the navigator divine!

A pickled map, a silly quest,
I zoom in close, but still can't guess.
Is that a hill or just a bump?
I twirl with laughter, not a dull chump.

Now a "recalculating" makes me pause,
Like a cat in a box, with no real cause.
Through winding ways and paths unseen,
I dance through life, the lost and the keen.

Pathways of the Heart

In love, they said, follow your bliss,
But I'm stuck in traffic—oh, is that a kiss?
The map looks vibrant, all colors and charms,
Yet I keep circling—are there hidden alarms?

A pathway blossoms, but it's a mirage,
On my GPS, I'm a lost little barrage.
Is that the café or just my old shoe?
I wish my heart had a clearer view!

Through a twisty alley, I find a stray cat,
It meows for my love, and that's something to chat!
But alas, dear feline, I'm on a quest,
To locate that heart that beats in my chest.

With landmarks of laughter and signs of surprise,
Every detour helps me improvise.
As I fumble and stumble, the compass spins,
Yet joy in the chaos, my adventure begins!

Unraveled Mysteries Beneath the Stars

Beneath the cosmos, I sought the hot spots,
But it led me to burgers, oh what a plot!
With every twinkling star, I swipe for a clue,
Yet all I find are headlights in view.

I follow Orion but stumble on Zeus,
A cosmic laugh, what a colorful ruse.
Are those deities lost, or am I just slow?
In this starlit quest, I'm a comical show!

Through tangled constellations, I search for a sign,
The Big Dipper spins 'round like a wobbly vine.
With each guide I trust, I end up in jest,
In the vast universe, I find my own fest.

So with my trusty GPS and dreams so bright,
I chart my own course by the moonlight.
Each wrong turn's a treasure, a gem to unfold,
In a galaxy quirky, hilarious, and bold!

The Silent Call of the Unknown

The road ahead whispers with mystery and flair,
But my GPS just giggles without a care.
Turn left at the rabbit, or right at the moon?
I'm driving in circles, a lost little loony!

With directions unclear and humor in tow,
I end up at Quirky Deli—oh, what a show!
The sign says 'all flavors', I'm game for that ride,
But should I trust a menu that's more like a guide?

Each turn that I take leads to laughter and cheer,
With sandwiches singing and jokes from the deer.
Oh, the dangers I've dodged—clowns, weird roads,
All the fun experiences lighten my loads.

In my whimsical journey, I know one true thing:
Though lost, I am found—let the giggling ring!
For in every detour, my heart finds its song,
In a world full of laughs, where I truly belong!

Mapping the Unmapped

In a world where I roam, the maps just confuse,
I've got a cute gadget, with choices to choose.
It asks for my route, then laughs with delight,
'I swear it's around here, just give me a bite!'

But the roads twist and turn, like a snake made of grass,
Tangled navigation, I'm fumbling, alas!
It says, 'Turn right at the donut,' oh heck,
But all I can find is a very lost trek!

I try to recalibrate, press buttons galore,
Yet I'm still navigating the wrong way to the store.
It's red on my screen, like a big warning sign,
But I'm hungry for tacos, just don't call me "divine".

So here's to the journey, and laughter galore,
With each wrong turn taken, I find even more.
For although I'm off track, and it seems quite absurd,
I still smile at life, with my trusty old bird.

A Search Within the Framework

I plugged in my home, but it showed me a cat,
Was this a mistake, or a clever old spat?
It says, 'In 300 feet, take a left at the wall,'
But all that I see is a spouting duck's call.

The framework is nifty; it gives me some cheer,
Yet somehow it leads me to places I fear.
Did it just giggle at my clueless despair?
I swear it suggested a trip to the fair!

Now I'm lost in a park where the dogs chase their tails,
While the GPS chuckles, crafting new trails.
It yells, 'Recalculate!' like a sarcastic mate,
I consider my options, yet cannot relate.

So maybe, just maybe, the path is the aim,
With each twist and turn, I'm defying the game.
For laughter's the true guide through this wacky ride,
And the framework of life gives joy I can't hide.

Circles in the Sky

My GPS showed me some circles in air,
'Is that a new route, or a cloud dream affair?'
It said, 'Continue straight,' but it circles me back,
Like a dog chasing tails, I'm lost on this track.

Up ahead, it points to some ducks and a slide,
'Is this the right path?' I question with pride.
They've taken the lead; I think I'll just wait,
I follow their quacks, in a twist of fate.

Around and around, in a dizzying spin,
The map just a jest, letting chaos begin.
But who needs a route when you've got a good laugh?
In the circles we wander, we choose our own path.

So let's dance in confusion, my feathered old friends,
With giggles and chuckles, we'll see where it ends.
For life is a journey, a riddle to scry,
I'm fine off the grid, in my circles up high.

Paths Woven by Fate

In my car with a map, I'm spinning my wheels,
While fate rolls her dice—how bizarre this feels!
It chirps at the corner, with wrong turns galore,
'You'll find wisdom in cookies!' Oh, what a chore.

As I sip my coffee, the road twists and bends,
Every detour I take is where humor transcends.
It lead me to laughter, and sights so outlandish,
Like a broccoli forest, all verdant and brandish.

Well, I meant to go north, but I stumbled on fate,
Who knew that a journey could feel so ornate?
With each sigh and hiccup, a chuckle erupts,
Life's GPS seems to delight in its flubs!

So here's to the trails that poke fun at my schemes,
The twists and the turns that feed wild, crazy dreams.
Be it cookies or broccoli, I'm glad for the fate,
For laughter's the fuel when you miss every gate.

Whispers from the Compass

The compass spins, a wild dance,
It seems to laugh, a foolish chance.
I point it east, it points me west,
  Is this a puzzle or just a jest?

A squirrel nods, 'You can't be lost!'
But here I am, I'm double-crossed.
The north star winks, the moon just sighs,
  Adventure calls, but where's the prize?

A map unfolds with minor flair,
But doodles made by kids declare,
A pirate's path, a dragon's den,
At least I've got my snacks and pen.

With every turn and every lane,
I question things that drive me insane.
Yet laughter echoes, and I roam,
In cosmic chaos, I find my home.

The Map of Forgotten Dreams

A map so old, it smells like dust,
Its secrets whispered can I trust?
A trail of crumbs leads to the past,
But wait! It's lunchtime, that'll be fast.

A dotted line, a wild goose chase,
Venison stew? Or ducky face?
I swap my compass for dessert,
And dream of wild trips, sugar alert!

Key to knowledge lies in crumbs,
Or is it just the sound of drums?
The X marks fun, not where to go,
At least my ice cream's on the show.

Forget the GPS, let's all yell,
To every glitch, there's a funny spell.
With every twist, I laugh and gleam,
Still lost, but found in an ice cream dream.

Journey Through Invisible Roads

Invisible roads that twist and twine,
Who knew the path could taste like wine?
The signs are shifty, a playful tease,
They lead me on with silly ease.

I follow arrows that blink and sway,
While "detour" signs just want to play.
A giraffe laughs as I take a turn,
With every mishap, a lesson learned.

Lost in laughter, I drive in circles,
Dodging potholes and playful turtles.
Cows in sunglasses cross the way,
In this crazy ride, I choose to stay.

With mischief and maps that play tricks,
I'll take the dips and rollercoaster licks.
Each wrong turn feels like a treat,
In this journey, I've found my beat.

The Quest for Clarity

In search of sense, I wear my specs,
But clarity's hiding, oh, what the heck?
A frog on the road croaks wisdom clear,
But translates poorly, oh dear, oh dear!

An owl advises, "Trust your own path,"
But follows me home, and there's a wrath.
With questions circling like barking hounds,
I trip on riddles, lost in bounds.

With every clue, I slip and slide,
Mental gymnastics take me for a ride.
But laughter breaks through, a sunny light,
As I dance through chaos, feeling just right.

Maps may mislead, but jokes are true,
Every mishap leads to something new.
So here I leap, with joy I'll frolic,
In the cosmic mess, I find the comic.

Aimless in the Wilderness

In a forest of confusion, I tread,
My compass spins round, it fled.
Trees wave their branches, they laugh and scoff,
"You'll find your way, just take a cough!"

A squirrel gives directions, so grand,
With nuts in his cheeks, he waves his hand.
"Just follow the creek, don't take a left,"
Yet I took the wrong path, I'm feeling bereft.

A butterfly flits, oh where can it be?
It flutters around mocking me with glee.
"Just use the map, it's all in the grid,"
But I'm way off course, oh, what a kid!

With every misstep, I enter the maze,
Chasing bad signals in a digital haze.
I laugh at the foolishness, let out a cheer,
At least I'm not lost…just delayed by a year!

The Coordinates of Desire

I punched in my dreams, a whimsical code,
To find my heart's treasure on this digital road.
But every turn leads to a hot dog stand,
Now craving mustard, oh fate's cruel hand!

I asked the GPS for a gourmet delight,
Instead, it guided me into a fight.
At a taco truck, with salsa so fierce,
My appetite danced, my senses it pierce.

Next, I set out for a café divine,
But ended up at a dog park, oh how unrefined!
Puppies caught my attention, what a surprise,
Now I'm left wondering which one to prize.

With each miscalculation, a lesson to glean,
Who knew happiness lies where you'd never been?
I chuckle at fate, it surely has flair,
A map is just paper if you've lost your care!

Lost in the Labyrinth of Thought

I've entered a maze of my own design,
Thoughts zigzagging wildly like a confused line.
Each corner I turn, there's a new surprise,
Like a piñata of worries, I cover my eyes!

I consulted my brain, like a wise old sage,
But it just chuckled, "You're stuck in a cage!"
Chasing after answers with fervor, I run,
But wisdom keeps hiding, oh isn't this fun?

A lightbulb flickers, then fizzles out fast,
Ideas like bubbles, they never last.
I grasp at my visions, they slip through my hands,
What a comical dance, with no real plans!

Yet in this grand tangle, I find a bright spark,
That laughter can shine in the depths of the dark.
So I tip my hat to this quirky old mind,
For every wrong turn, there's joy to find!

Navigating Shadows

I'm lost in a world where shadows collide,
As I wander the alleys where secrets reside.
Every turn brings a ghost; it giggles away,
As I fumble for daylight, nearly lose my sway.

Monsters of doubt rear their heads in the night,
But I laugh at them deeply and put up a fight.
With the moon as my guide, I dance through the gloom,
Creating a party in the silence of doom!

I asked a shadow for directions clear,
It just winked at me, whispered, "Never fear!"
For life is a puzzle, both whimsical and weird,
And getting lost is the best thing I've cheered.

So here's to the wanderers, the dreamers at heart,
Navigating shadows is a curious art.
With laughter our compass, we'll find our own way,
In this fuzzy twilight, we'll seize the day!

Fragments of a Greater Journey

I typed in a place, my phone took a chance,
It led me in circles, a confusing dance.
I waved to a duck, thought it might be a guide,
But all it did was quack, and then it just tried.

I asked it for coffee, but it sent me afar,
To a shop that served tea in a tin can jar.
A route to adventure, it promised in text,
Only to find out I ended up vexed.

It said, 'In three miles, a treasure awaits,'
But all that I found were some old rusty skates.
With every wrong turn, I laughed at my fate,
It seems life's best mapped by the whims of a mate.

So here on this journey, I'll take it in stride,
For every wrong turn is a wild, fun ride.
With giggles and grins, I'll dance down this road,
And find joy in the chaos, that's how it's bestowed.

Echoes of an Invisible Map

There's a compass inside that doesn't comply,
It points not to north, but to blueberry pie.
My quest leads me sideways, I've lost track of time,
Each corner I turn feels like a nursery rhyme.

"Recalculate now!" the voice chirps with glee,
While I chase a raccoon that just stole my key.
It winks as it darts, like a slick little thief,
While I hop on one leg, yelling, "Give it back, chief!"

In a van down by rivers, I pull up a seat,
For a nap or a snack, on this mysterious beat.
The map's full of squiggles, leading me astray,
But laughter echoes louder than getting the way.

So here I will linger, in this whimsical whirl,
As stars sprinkle wisdom, in this timeless twirl.
Though it's all just a game, I'll take every chance,
For life has a rhythm, and I'll take the dance.

The Intersection of Fate and Frequency

The GPS chimes, like a singing bird,
But I want to tune to some otherword.
'At the next light, make a u-turn,' it pleads,
Yet my heart says, 'Stay, plant some wild seeds.'

I found myself wandering, laughing aloud,
Dancing with shadows, drawing my crowd.
The route led to nowhere, or perhaps to the skies,
Guess it's not the path, but the moments that rise.

There's a coffee shop pushing the limits of time,
With lattes that spark like a nonsensical rhyme.
"Is this place on the map?" I yell to the crew,
"The menu's a riddle, let's solve it anew!"

Through detours and hiccups, I savor the trip,
For getting lost sometimes gives life a good grip.
So I map out my laughter, and I dance on this spree,
In the frequency of fun, I find serenity.

Directions Scribbled in the Sand

The shoreline swirls like a magical tale,
I drew lines in the sand with a watery trail.
With a clump of seaweed, I made an 'X',
But the tide came in faster than I could text.

"Time to reroute," my phone said with flair,
As I dodged crabs dancing, caught in their snare.
I followed a seashell that looked somewhat wise,
It whispered directions and laughed at my sighs.

With footprints behind me, I boldly declared,
That getting lost here feels wonderfully rare.
Each wave that rolled in was a wink from the sea,
A reminder that joy is the only decree.

So I'll dig up the treasures, let the sun light my way,
For the journey's the prize, come what may!
And through every misstep, I'll find my own tune,
In the sand of my heart, I'll dance to the moon.

Footprints in Digital Sand

I typed in my quest, to find my lost shoe,
But ended up at a café with a great view.
My GPS laughed, 'You really can't steer,
Food's the best treasure you'll find just near.'

I followed the blue dot, it danced on the screen,
Took me on a jaunt through a park so green.
Chasing my map like a squirrel on a spree,
Lost in the bushes - is that a lost tree?

The landmarks are quirky, and roads go askew,
With every wrong turn, I found something new.
A llama in sneakers, a cat with a bow,
My route to adventure just goes where I flow.

So forget about distance, and just take a ride,
With giggles and snacks, I'll cruise far and wide.
Those footprints in digital sand fade away,
But the laughs and the stories? They'll forever stay.

Between the Lines of Each Map

A map on my phone told me where to go,
But why it leads me to a circus, I don't know.
With clowns juggling pickles and bears riding bikes,
I grin at the chaos, am I here for the sights?

The streets are all wobbly, like gum on a shoe,
Each step of my journey a wacky debut.
I skip past the signs that say, 'Turn left at fun',
Adventure's my compass, I'm never quite done.

In the middle of nowhere, there's more to explore,
A treasure map showing me jellybean lore.
I pause just a moment, to dance on the spot,
Between the lines of each map, I'll give it a shot.

So, onward I wander, not just bricks and stone,
With laughter and whimsy, I'll never be lone.
For every missed exit and unintended ride,
Leads to hilarious tales I can't help but confide.

Compass Rose in a Stormy Sky

My compass is spinning, what's north anyway?
The clouds above giggle, it's all a grand play.
The wind gives a shout, 'Just follow me now!'
But up ahead, I see a cow, oh wow!

It's mooing with glee, a true cartographer,
Mapping the fields like a playful conjurer.
'Turn left for the fries, then right for a shake,
Maps can be tricky, but oh what a break!'

I dodge puddles of mud like a ballet star,
With ducks as my audience, I'm off to the bar.
Each flip of my compass brings giggles anew,
A storm overhead, but I'm laughing right through.

So bring on the storms, let the raindrops dance,
With every wild turn, I just take a chance.
In the chaos around, a compass can bark,
Leading me home to a light in the dark.

The Longest Detour

Detouring over hills, oh what a delight,
With my phone as my guide, I'm lost but alright.
The road signs point onward, but I'm in a maze,
'A ten-minute drive' turns into a week's phase.

The loop-de-loops take me on twists and turns,
Finding offbeat attractions, oh how my heart yearns.
A giant rubber chicken, an ice cream parade,
I might be a bit lost, but memories are made.

My car's like a turtle, moving so slow,
With laughter around me, there's always a show.
Who needs to be timely when adventure is grand?
The longest detour can lead you by hand.

So flip the direction, let chaos refine,
In this funny old journey, I'll always be fine.
Here's to missed exits and spirits so bright,
In the land of the detour, everything's right!

www.ingramcontent.com/pod-product-compliance
Lightning Source LLC
Chambersburg PA
CBHW071844160426
43209CB00003B/408